Pet Care

# Cats

Dash!
LEVELED READERS
An Imprint of Abdo Zoom • abdobooks.com

1

# Dash!
## LEVELED READERS

### Level 1 – Beginning
Short and simple sentences with familiar words or patterns for children who are beginning to understand how letters and sounds go together.

### Level 2 – Emerging
Longer words and sentences with more complex language patterns for readers who are practicing common words and letter sounds.

### Level 3 – Transitional
More developed language and vocabulary for readers who are becoming more independent.

**abdobooks.com**

Published by Abdo Zoom, a division of ABDO, PO Box 398166, Minneapolis, Minnesota 55439.
Copyright © 2019 by Abdo Consulting Group, Inc. International copyrights reserved in all countries.
No part of this book may be reproduced in any form without written permission from the publisher.
Dash!™ is a trademark and logo of Abdo Zoom.

Printed in the United States of America, North Mankato, Minnesota.
092018
012019

Photo Credits: iStock, Shutterstock
Production Contributors: Kenny Abdo, Jennie Forsberg, Grace Hansen, John Hansen
Design Contributors: Dorothy Toth, Neil Klinepier

Library of Congress Control Number: 2018945933

## Publisher's Cataloging in Publication Data

Names: Murray, Julie, author.
Title: Cats / by Julie Murray.
Description: Minneapolis, Minnesota : Abdo Zoom, 2019 | Series: Pet care |
    Includes online resources and index.
Identifiers: ISBN 9781532125201 (lib. bdg.) | ISBN 9781641856652 (pbk) |
    ISBN 9781532126222 (ebook) | ISBN 9781532126734 (Read-to-me ebook)
Subjects: LCSH: Domestic cats--Juvenile literature. | Cats--Behavior--Juvenile
    literature. | Pets--Juvenile literature.
Classification: DDC 636.8--dc23

# Table of Contents

# Cats

Cats make great pets. They need safe homes to roam around.

Cats need fresh food and water every day. Some cats like dry food. Others like wet food. Mittens likes both!

Cats need a litter box. This is where they go to the bathroom. It needs to be kept clean.

Cats need toys. They like to play. They like to climb and jump too! Patches plays with the toy mouse.

11

Cats have sharp claws. They need a place where they can scratch. A scratching post is a good thing to have in your house.

Cats are clean animals. They **groom** themselves. Their tongue acts like a hairbrush. They use their paws to clean areas their tongue can't reach.

Cats **communicate** with sound. They meow loudly when they want attention or are hungry. They purr softly when they are **content**.

Cats need to see a **veterinarian**. This keeps them healthy. Boots gets his check-up.

Cats sleep a lot. Some
cats sleep 18 hours a day!
Sammy sleeps in the sun
by the window.

# Things Cats Need

- Food and water

- A litter box

- Toys to play with

- A scratching post

# Glossary

**communicate** – to express one's feelings.

**content** – comfortable and happy.

**groom** – to make clean and neat.

**veterinarian** – a doctor for animals.

# Index

# Online Resources

**Booklinks**
**NONFICTION NETWORK**
**FREE!** ONLINE NONFICTION RESOURCES

To learn more about cat care, please visit **abdobooklinks.com**. These links are routinely monitored and updated to provide the most current information available.